*Lights
in the
Constellation
of the
Crab*

Angus D.H. Ogilvy

Published by Hermit Crab,
30/5 Polwarth Crescent Edinburgh EH11 1HN
hermitcrabpoems@gmail.com

Poems © Angus D.H. Ogilvy 2012

ISBN # 978-0-9572764-0-6

All rights reserved

The moral right of the author has been asserted

The author gives Maggie's Centres the right to print copies of this book or reproduce individual poems as required by them as long as the author is acknowledged.

Final Consultation first appeared in the anthology *Nothing left to burn* by Ragged Raven Press 2011

Set in Gentium Book Basic
Printed by printondemand-worldwide

Front Cover: Julia Krone Oliver, **Constellation**, oil on board, 40x40 cms
Back Cover: detail from Julia Krone Oliver, **Constellation**
www.juliakrone.com
Photographed by Michael Wolchover
www.michael-wolchover.com

Acknowledgements:
Thanks to Valerie Gillies for her skill and generosity in editing this book, Julia Krone Oliver for her beautiful painting, and to Michael Wolchover for donating his special photographic expertise.

All proceeds from this book go directly to Maggie's Cancer Caring Centres

Words from Andrew Anderson, Maggie's Edinburgh:

We are absolutely delighted that Angus has been able to support Maggie's by publishing a collection of his poems. Angus has inspired and uplifted all who have had the pleasure of hearing and reading his poetry within Maggie's Edinburgh and now a wider audience have the opportunity to share the wisdom, eloquence and humour through this book. He has beautifully embraced Maggie's programme of support and has given back more than he will realise. We hope others are inspired to take part in and enjoy the Creative Writing Course at Maggie's. It continues to be a genuine pleasure for all of us to know Angus and his family.

Contents

Gatherings	8
Cartography	9
Splenomegaly	10
Edge	14
First Screening	15
Not the Story	16
When They Told Me	17
ward window	18
Connotations of the Big C	19
Purification	20
In the Grand Scale of Things	21
Autumn Gale	22
In a Word	23
New Blood	24
How Long?	25
Song of the Chemo Dispenser	26
Within	27
On His Baldness	28
A Small Matter of Refreshment	29
Opening and Closing	30
Gentle Man Jim	31
As Moon	32
White Out	33
Homage to Blackford Hill	34
Oncology Lift	35
Data Capture	35
Death	36
Cancer Ward 8	37
Lawn Tennis Association	38
A Night on the TPN	39
Death is So Much Closer Now in Digital 3D	40

Identity Tag	41
To You Who Are Well	42
Well	43
Raised Eyebrows	44
Coruscation	45
Coonsel	46
Shock of the Expected	47
Ever Since	48
Calling	49
Transplanted	50
Chemo and the Emerging Follicles	51
After the Treatment	52
Memo to Myself, Living	53
Remission	54
In Plain View	54
Chemo Brain	55
Chemo Brain: Appointment	55
Out of the Passive Voice	56
Gratitude for Whatever	57
The World We Have	58
At Oldshoremore	59
No Hero	60
Just a Check Up	61
State of the Art	62
That's the Point	63
Final Consultation	64

Foreword

In 2008 while working in Africa, I was diagnosed in the advanced stages of Non-Hodgkin Mantle Cell Lymphoma. In hindsight I suppose the signs had been there, but at the time they certainly didn't add up in my mind to anything of such gravity, the default position of many a Scottish male. All around me, it seemed, people were dealing with much greater challenges in their lives.

On returning to Edinburgh, I began treatment at the Western General with a medical team in whom I had great confidence and with the unfailing support of my family, friends, and the new 'family' I was introduced to at Maggie's Centre. There I was given comfort, clarity, copious cups of tea and the confidence to look into this experience and articulate it through my writing in the hope that it might be of some benefit to others living with the intensity of the processes of cancer. It is not a journey I would have chosen, but since it has chosen me, it continues to be one that offers me powerful human experience and inspiration.

All of these poems came from my new life with cancer. Some stand on their own without that cancer lens, and sometimes, like the first poem, *Gatherings*, their connection with 'the emperor of all maladies' only became apparent after they were written.

My gratitude to the team at Maggie's Edinburgh is immense and this collection is some small way to express it.

May you be well!

Lights in the Constellation of the Crab

To Carol and Neil,
my friends at Maggie's,
and all my teachers through word or example.

The expectations I expected
were not the expectations
I expected them to be.

Angus D.H. Ogilvy

Gatherings

The birds are coming now
in flocks,
gathering night
in huddles of darkness,
swirling above spent fields
where pools of sky
solidify on seals of ice.

They come for sanctuary,
perhaps,
or refuge, with their conformations
of disorder, elegant equations
for the chaos of the crowd,
swaddling eggshell air
with press of presence.

They are lost to multitudes,
subsumed
by purposes beyond control,
reacting to some flicker
of a neighbour's eye he does not know,
that sweeps them spiralling
along one final flitting plume of light.

Cartography

Following the old maps, he arrived
just where he had planned to be.
The landscape conformed to interpretation:
that hill, those clumps of trees, the village gathered
around the bridge. He saw the things
he'd expected to see, given the forecasts,
the time of year: the lone fox and the raven falling.

He wasn't prepared for the motorbike
coming screaming round where the road forked right
in a curving descent over spreading contours
to the valley floor. Nothing could indicate how to turn
avoiding oblivion, the uncharted plunge,
the way time stretched through the flick of an eye
to a sound and a light in a circling loop;
but he did.

Splenomegaly

The body has a lump.

The lump is growing.

Just under the rib cage
on the left side reaching down.

A torn muscle;
too many sit-ups rippling my abdomen.

And yet no pain.
No pain at all.

And weight loss too.
Yes.

But no surprise
after all that walking, swimming,
my modest diet.

Night sweats?
Well, of course.
The time of year!
The male menopause!

The spleen is considerably enlarged.

The spleen?
Funny.
Funny how you need to be alerted to the spleen's existence.
Heart, lungs, liver, kidneys – you know of them.

Even the pancreas and the bitter gall.

What does the spleen do anyway?
And where exactly should it be?
Spleens rupture – don't they?

Yes, but this is not a ruptured spleen.
The spleen helps to clean the blood.
It is part of the immune system.

Then why is it so big and hard?

I cannot discount lymphoma.

Lymphoma.

What a lovely word!
A place in Montana.
A child's soft drink.
A moonlit orchid.

Why do I feel a frisson of fear along my spine?

You've probably been carrying this cancer
In your system for some time.

Cancer.

He said cancer.

I see the word
and all its letters have soft curves.
Only the first sound cracks

hard in the skull like a splenetic Viking's hammer.
Hard as my spleen.

And yet if you cut it out,
eradicate that *K*,
you are left only with the softness
of the...answer.

So what now?

We cure it.

Cure it.
Like a dead pig into ham.
No ifs, no buts,
straight to the spleen of the matter.

I am grateful for that compassionate directness;
the confidence of hope.

First let us do some tests to be sure we know
exactly what we are dealing with.
Then we will cure it.

How?

A regimen of chemotherapy.
And then, perhaps, a stem cell transplant.

I see a line of cells with roots
taking hold, multiplying.
These things have come a long way
in the past few years.

*New drugs! Better drugs!
It is not the terrible vomiting mess
you may imagine from all you've heard before.
Many don't even lose their hair!*

I run my hand through my beard.

*If you need to talk to anyone
about anything concerning this,
my door is always open.*

Thank you, doctor, I appreciate it.

And I really do.

I walk out through the open door
into the radiance of a high veldt afternoon:
the flame trees and the flowers;
a hoopoe bobbing on the lawn.

The beauty of it overflows inside me,
smartens my eyes.

No ifs, no buts.
I have a purpose.

I have awakened from a long, long sleep
and from this moment
I will be
alive.

Edge

You never know where you might find your edge,
and, spun by vertigo, flail to grasp
the crumbling earth, snatching at sparse
scrub wedged by twisted roots for rootless legs,
jarring the panic wilding of the heart
to sudden stillness.
                      Then, how to move from
that tight, cold spot; exposed, alone, remote,
hemmed between yawning emptiness - the space
of the possible – and the tyranny of place?

For this is the test. It doesn't matter
that it struck as you'd hardly begun to
feel those slopes beneath your feet, or after
turning from the top for the long descent;
it's how you will open, what your intent.

First Screening

So what is the cause of the symptoms?

*We've made an initial investigation,
but the full extent of the condition
isn't yet clear; it's not an exact science.
We do see cellular mutation masked by
viral or bacterial infection,
but such results give no indication
of a specific cause or reason why.*

I watch the jacaranda shed a leaf;
something unremarkable and brief
in the long unfolding of earth and seed
to violet flower where fat bees feed:
forked lightning struck its branches from the dark,
and termites tunnel, blind, beneath its bark.

Not The Story

No, not me!
This is not the story
I had promised me to be:
a character re-crafted
into someone else's play,
the one you see
declining to a pre-determined end.

It's not me, friend.
No, no.
It's you.

My story never went this way.
It had me firm on solid ground,
no indication that the rock was sand;
a life-light radiant in my hands
revealing paths without,
within.

No, not me!
It isn't me.
It's him:
plucked away by circumstances,
carried off by whim.

It doesn't have projected glory.

Sorry.
Must be someone else's story.

When They Told Me
(for Maggie's Cancer Caring Centre)

When they told me,
earth transformed to water;
water, in a rush of air,
dissolved to space.

All around were nurseries of fire:
the lonely angers of the burning self
that could not look on failing
with a mother's eyes
and understand it didn't matter.

Through glass, I watched the process
of the chemistries of change;
observed its deformations, reformations;
saw the way things strived to re-arrange,
now that I had left me
to the mercy of its own devices.

Maggie's found me,
I found *Maggie's*,
re-introduced us with a mug of lemon tea,
the gentle cheer of knowing, feeling,
seeing there was yet an I that could,
despite the poor prognosis,
purposefully engage with me.

ward window

toxic elixir
from the black cloaked bag
drips on

the sallow moon
a lemon slice
on the ripening bruise of dawn

snow clouds sliding south
on dying winds

hills like mammoths
cowering for warmth

sunburst comes
with glancing gems on window panes
an arriving plane a comet without omen

the giant beech
that's reaching up into the frame
holds other trees in twigs and branches
trees within trees
the same

Connotations of the Big C

Cancer: the tropic of…

Cancer: the topic of… abnormal cellular conformation:

    conversation
    consultation
    contemplation
    confirmation
    consternation
    confrontation
    condemnation
    consecration
    conflagration
    consolation

Cancer: the constellation of…

Crab: any of numerous ten-footed crustaceans
        having the first pair of legs modified as

        pin Cers

Purification

Eyes shut,
I visualise light.

It enters the crown
and down, down, down
through every body part
and pore, the membrane wall
of each formed cell,
and fills them all
with brilliance.

Crabs crawl
from hidden places,
scramble sideways
from the glare
down, down deep;
they throng through holes
and the soles of my feet
into the warm earth's
darkness.

It should be sea
I send them to,
the cleansing of salt,
these green crustaceans
far from their oceans
hatching from the marrow
of my bones.

But I am of earth;
its season turning,

turning to living
from death's decay
in light I offer
to the lengthening day.

They will bury themselves
under roots of trees,
crevices the earth has opened
to receive
this quiet seeding
of my disease.

In the Grand Scale of Things

The dying are
still living.

The living are
still dying.

Life is a frangible balance of forces.

The dead
are sometimes alive.

The alive
are sometimes dead.

Autumn Gale

The north wind
wills to lift my frail frame like a kite;
its single purpose forged
in salted maelstroms over Faeroe.

I push my boots down hard
against the earth;
my trousers flap like unroped jibs
around the battered reef knots of my knees;
my jacket thrashing south south east;
my skull white-knuckled
in the tension of its grip.

I wonder
should I just let go,
unjam the cleats
and let the body fly
in these fleet forces
so much greater than my own;
to vanish on the freak gusts
of the gale?

Or would I then be tossed
and shredded like a bin bag
flayed on railings
rattling my last breaths away?

No fear.

Only resistance
turns the kite

meticulous upon the air;
tugging dogged life
from cane and canvas
with a string;
making elemental forces
sing.

In a Word

You're mortal.
Yes!
I'm alive;
something I share with countless billion.

You're terminal.
No!
That can't be right.
I demand a second opinion!

You're clear.
You see!
There's plenty life left
in this old dog yet!

You're in remission.
So,
it's lurking there,
waiting;
and I can't forget.

New Blood

The infusion machines ring
like electronic icicles
dripping in a bowl of synthesized air.

Someone else's blood
is flushing through
the back of my hand.

Strange to be merged
with an unknown other:
Donation Number: G101 608 802 614F.

Now
whose bruises will I bear?
Whose shame or anger flush the cheeks?
Whose dread will drain the vessels of this face?
Whose anticipation thrum these ears?
Whose love assault the tight pump of the heart?

Interconnection made manifest
by that scarlet bag that drains
another's life blood through the veins
of recipient CHI 110 541 293;
the previously imagined
me.

How Long?

How long have I got?
I asked the keeper of truths
now that I lived in the shadow of days.

How long do you need,
the keeper replied:
eternity; a month; an allotted span
long enough for you to arrive
at the moment when nothing remains to achieve;
or a little more now, and a little more then?

The fall of a feather;
a bend in the river;
the print of a life at the heart of a stone;
the rings in a yew tree;
the sound of a star at the birth of the universe;
dispersal of smoke from the fire in my grate;
the drying-out wings of the dragonfly waking,
stretching and trembling to feel it is here.

I turned from the keeper
who sat in my shadow,
paid my respects
and opened the door.

Song of the Chemo Dispenser*

Oh he
        llo!
Red lights
        glow.
Here we
        go!
Please, god,
        no!
High and
        low.
No more
        flow.
Tensions
        grow.
Grow and
        grow!
Going to
        blow!

Had my
        dose.
I sup
        pose
No one
        knows.
No one
        shows.
Systems
        froze.
Lachry
        mose

Chemo
        woes!

Oh! Oh!
        Oh!
Oh! Oh!
        Oh!
Oh! Oh!
        Oh!
Oh! Oh!
        Oh!
Oh! Oh!
        Oh!
Oh! Oh!
        Oh!

Oh for god's sake, would somebody just stick a flush in it
before it sends me right off my trolley!

* this poem can be intoned to the notes GG D, the song of the chemo dispenser

Within

Look into it, look in:
the terror in the tiger's eye,
the trembling of the djinn,
the frightened blood of tyranny
that's circling within.

Begin with it.
Look into it, look into it;
look in!

On His Baldness

The chemistry turned
all my follicles void.
I knew I'd be bald;
I can't be annoyed.

No hair to wash, well
one less thing to do:
time saved on preening
and choosing shampoo,

Or plucking of eyebrows
that grow the wrong way
and rogue hairs on nipples
as long as the day.

Long barren nostrils
don't gather up snot,
so nothing to pick
when lost in a thought.

There's something quite pure
in the bareness of toes,
or armpits and fingers
where nothing more grows.

The cock is not lost
like a mushroom in grass
and nothing gets ripped
when wiping my arse.

So goodbye to barbers;

a fortune to save!
and throw out the razor;
there's f... all to shave!

I'll take on the world as
bare as a baby!
Authentically naked!
That's me! Well....maybe.

A Small Matter of Refreshment

Lunch in Ward 8.

Hello doll!
Dae ye want some milk wi' yer dinner?
Green semi skimmed or blue full fat?
Or dis it matter?

And on the carton is a label:

Jacob M.
Extras Ward 08
15/01/2009
Milk 250 ml F/C
RETURN IF UNUSED.

I guess it disnae matter.

Opening and Closing

Opening is the only way:

giving the guards extended leave;
calling off the dogs;
cutting down the razor wires;
springing the man traps;
dowsing the beacon fires;
releasing the jailed demons;

and letting the self fall back
into the buoyancy bag
it lacked the faith to be there;

then absorbing and emitting light
that weeps through pores to circle suffering
from which it tried so long in vain
to quarantine the dread of pain.

Opening is the only way:

closing is an invitation
to more ingenious violation –
those rounds of action and inaction it requires
forever after, feeding on aversion and desire.

Opening is the only way:

closing's just a gallant gesture
with plated armour, sharpened sword,
jousting with the courage word
that roots in fear.

No, it is clear,
opening is the only way.

For, in the end, there's nothing,
nothing to defend except deception,
my shadow truth,
that fatal flaw of false perception.

Gentle Man Jim

Jim's my phlebotomist; he takes my bloods.
He proudly detects the faintest of thuds
in my pulse, then slips in his needle
without any fuss or need to fiddle,
or - even worse - miss and cause me pain
and do the procedure all over again.

He works with the stealth of a gentleman mugger.
Jim's not your average bloody vein bugger.

As Moon

A long sweep passing since
I saw the moon
as moon.

The flare of summer,
town horizons,
cloud-cast sky ways;
all the moot excuses
I assume.

I see it now

moon as moon

gravid with harvest

rising in the crisping
of a fading afternoon.

White-out

How can this be? I've walked here too often.
I know the hollows and undulations,
the stub of each culled tree, the abrasions
on scuffed stones, slopes where desire-lines soften,
every wind-scent on its open spaces.

Now it enfolds me, without horizon,
spidered in a bowl I strain my eyes on,
stung by wind-smacked snow, searching for traces
of anything I know; blinded by white,
trapped by panic, memory holds no key;
my footfalls - vanished; my only birthright
where I stand, sinking, and finally free
of knowing anything but I am here,
so very, very far, yet still so near.

Homage to Blackford Hill

Beautiful blunt plug of igneous,
I calibrate myself against
your bluff sides
by the nuance of my breath
through clutching lungs;
the bloodbeat haemoglobin
in the thrumming of my head;
the leverage that sets
the spring and balance of my legs
against your better inclinations.
My monitor of vim.
My pressure gauge.
My sure pulsometer.

No tourniquets or tubes.
No pumps or sensors.
No vials or hypodermics.
Just unencumbered
steps through whindrift
on prevailing winds
that tease me always upwards
with your more and more revealing
panoramic points of view.

Or test me
with the stamina of flowers
caught in the clamp
of winter's hardened ways,
persisting where I'd known
they could not grow.

Oncology Lift

Doors opening
Stage 1
Going up
Doors closing

Doors opening
Stage 2
Going up
Doors closing

Doors opening
Stage 3
Going up
Doors closing.

Doors opening
Stage 4
Going down
Doors closing

Data Capture

The dead can be recorded without fuss.
It's tough to keep track of the ones who live:
who to accept and who to reject.
Some won't follow up, so there's never enough.

I suppose the best advice I can give
is to be a statistic that's hard to collect.

Death

Oh death,
you scare the living shit out of me
in your grotesque disguises.

But I don't expect to find you
with a sting graven on the hoo-ha
of your self-proclaimed victory.

Everywhere you are imaged
as the grim, unavoidable obstacle:
dark lord, cloaked reaper, skull dancer.

I see the horrors pinned to your gate
and snigger at those self-indulgent poster boys
of misspent youth you've placed there.

Up close and personal
underneath that cracking make-up
you're as soft as leftover flesh
after the revelling spirits have departed.

It's a dead end job, I know,
acting out a persona that's just not you
for the sake of those who know not
who or what you really are, and would do
what they could to deny you thrice,
in the dark before the dawn.

So, for a silver shilling,
you play the role of reluctant host
at this creaking gate you open

to admit my spell of breathing into light,
at the easing of a short pupation
in preparation for rainbow flight.

Cancer Ward 8

In the wee small hours
pain splatters profanities
through the tube of his throat,
smacking us from slumber.

Ah! Ah! AAHH!
JESUS FUCKING CHRIST!
Can ye no DAE SOMETHING?
GOD ALL FUCKING MIGHTY!
AH! AH! AAHH!
DAE SOMETHING!

PLEASE!

All our anger,
all our hate,
all our sorrow
surges through him
in defiance of the darkness.

And for him too
a light will penetrate
the fontanelle of his naked skull
and fill him with milk and honey
vital as morphine.

Lawn Tennis Association

I can't watch tennis any more
without the nag of needles
and the forty love fault
one set down of bolused bitters
candying my veins with Wimbledon Rock:

the strawberry knock
                       knock
                                  knock
gasp
      clapping
                    tie break
                                          uproar of applause
through tubes
         advantage
                        deuce
while lying on the broken serve of sleep
rebellious without a cause
and challenging the umpire in the heat,
or racked by racket rhythms on the pulse,
pass
      smash
            and volley
backhand cannulated drop-shot dripping
line-call trolley
            ball-boy all attached,

waiting for a last
                  game,
                            set,
                                      and match!

A Night on the TPN*

You could see that the treatment had taken its toll,
but his wit was resilient and vital and whole,
and he'd honed it as sharp as a samurai's sword
when he came from the unit back into the ward.

His pièce de résistance and crowning glory
was the night that he dined on a hospital story:
not able to swallow, his system being down,
they came into his room with a night on the town.

*A bloody great bag was hooked up tae ma vein.
And I'm hopin' I don't see the likes o't again!
Seven hundred quid for one bloody meal,
and ye can only enjoy it when ye're no feelin' weel!*

*It was the dearest damned meal that I've ever had.
But that's no the best bit, ye understand:
they had ham and egg flavour or haddock and chips,
but nae table service, so, ergo, nae tips!*

*Total Parenteral Nutrition

Death is So Much Closer Now in Digital 3D *

So it's confirmed, then.
Positive.

Well, negative.
A negative positive.

Shocked!
I mean, who wouldn't be:
wondering which way?

You feel, yes, yes, you feel, you must!

What to do with all those
sensuous images you'd stored away
of what things should be like
some other day?

It hurts; being altered.

Like a sudden meteor
you're falling, falling
into other people's air:

the discomfort of strangers
struggling to find the words to say;
and thinking, could they just but turn,
turn and look the other way.

Besides, what was that about:
those old routines of living
in the memory of what future

ought to be?

They'll be wondering
what you did to deserve it,
yes, they'll be wondering.
Did you *do* something to bring it on?
In you they will reflect again
their personal aspirations.
You'll burden them to reconfigure
all the inconveniences they've labelled sane.

You'll be their reminder of the tremor of reality,
the insubstantial mist of certainty,
the rising of the surge, the wild wind's roar,
the boiling, roiling turmoil of the sea,
the unframed thought, the drowning instant,
the blood-rush pounding surf come closer,
closer, so much closer now in digital 3D:

closer, closer, my god, to thee.

*(Title taken from an ad on the side of an Edinburgh bus)

Identity Tag

You can tell who we are
by the badges we wear;
we're *The Bloods* – see it there
on our arms like a scar,
or tattoo in the shape
to mark those from the camp,
haematology's stamp:
lump of cotton, ripped tape.

To You Who Are Well

Listen.

Let us escape from
the cages of your guilt for living,
and forgetting to live;

The bars you've built in greenery and stone
with all that sadness of yourselves
that you would also die unshriven,
and how you cannot own to it;

The thoughts that haunt
and hunt you now in the vulnerable shadows
underneath the trees where water
makes no sound,
but passes, slides forever on.

You are not,
nor ever will be,
in control.

Let go.

Let go of your neat garden of desires,
your carefully ordered allotments of wishes
with all their cultivated, crafted forms.

Come with me now and enter
this untended glade that's domed by song,
its fierce light filtered through relentless layers of dust:
our dust.

And we will never rush again,
or strive for breathless destinations
where, once arrived, we'd bend ourselves
to forming new itineraries.

Nor shall we reminisce, fruitlessly.
For now there will be nothing to promote,
no leafless causes to defend against the sky.

Only, we shall walk and sit,
and feel the pungent weightiness of wild garlics
lifting,
giving way to primroses;
while all these mosses over fallen walls
would gather up their sheens.

Well

At the window which
never gets sun
an icicle
drips:

weep
now.

Raised Eyebrows

More than anything else, more even than
the promise of cure, he wanted eyebrows.

He'd noticed how they noticed him, the old ones,
smiled in under-voices to his dad:
How's he doing, poor wee mite? Such a sin.
The wig was as good as a head full of hair:
they never gave *it* a second glance;
but when they caught the full shock of his eyes
beneath those empty arches, set, intense,
they'd jar theirs into masks of caught concern.

When the lady with the make-up made her rounds,
she looked, and with her pencil drew a wish
that granted him the curvature of wings
on which he'd glide above those wonderings.

Coruscation

Light accentuates dark.

In winter dawns
I turn on my lamp
and morning rolls over to midnight.

Dark accentuates light.

Relinquishing gloom
I am dazzled
by the lustre of the universe.

It doesn't matter that
the house burns down in the night
in a pre-emptive attack on murk.

It doesn't matter that
hope's slim candle splutters
in its see-saw dance with dread.

Only my light,
which accentuates
and is accentuated by dark,
shall pass.

Coonsel

Go on.

Dae yersel a favour.
Get aff yer hump
an' smile fur god's sake!

There.

Ye see!

It's no that bad efter a',
well is it?

It is!

Ah see!

Well if ah wis you
ah widnae be lookin'
sae bloody smug aboot it!

Shock of the Expected

It was as good
as something like that could be.

The children came
the day before
and they had lunch together.

The sun shone well enough
to let them sit in the garden
out of the wind.

He enjoyed the play
of light in the trees.

That night
his mother rang
and they had a nice long chat.

He didn't wake in the morning
and it seems he hadn't suffered in the night.

Even though they knew it would happen,
they didn't expect it
quite so soon.

Ever Since

Ever since she said she's dying,
I see hearses.

She isn't dying any more urgently
than before;

but there are more hearses
glimpsed at corners,
between green pillars,
passing the ends of aisles
in second-hand bookshops,
waiting at crossings.

They glide over shivering stones.
Sometimes there are flowers;
sometimes polished emptiness,
my reflection,
the after-taste of ozone.

Calling

There has to be a calling here:

changing the incontinent's sheets;

staunching the panic of blood
when the lymphomaniac
rips the cannula from his vein;

cleaning cytotoxic waste
spilled from the burst colostomy bag;

untangling the knots of pain
around a pent up passion of abuse.

And then the constant vigilance:
the checking and rechecking
of dosages and drugs, the vital signs,
surfing on the metronomes of digital infusions.

Or tending dissolution into death;
the insufficient end of something filed,
but never fully understood.

This is no contractual obligation,
doling reimbursement by the daub
of sterile swab on flaking skin.

For those who spend their nights and days
assuaging cancer's terminal fear,
there has to be a calling here.

Transplanted

Beached
on a new shore,
my bottle with no message,
where crabs race between waves.

A monitor emerges from the sea
flicking its senses over me,
but finding no signs of life
or death
shuffles on towards the possibilities
of fallen figs.

So here I lie under another sun,
washed of old dependencies,
on a swathe bounded by rocks
between earth and space,
land and sea,
on the edge of mighty evolutions;

held by the mingling of fate
and the relentless tide of Charles Darwin.

Chemo and the Emerging Follicles

My stubbly face has the look of neglect,
long lost ambition, self-disrespect,
an abandoned field when harvest has gone,
the rough edge of life to be grating upon.
And grating will garner a gobful of trouble;
that's what you get with a faceful of stubble.

Stubble's rejection, the bent to rebel!
People look sideways, sniff for the smell,
expectant of put-downs, objections to life:
He's not got a razor, but where is the knife?
Van Gogh cut his ear off to murder his pain:
he had grown stubble, he was insane!

Put down your judgements! Something's afoot!
Where once I was bald, I am turning hirsute.
What you see here is a faceful of hope,
for what is now rough was once smooth as soap.
A roguish rebirth from a velvety bubble,
I gasp in the glory of rasping sharp stubble!

After the Treatment

'You look so *well!*'

What else can you say?

'You *look* so well!'

Does it matter that
you can't see the decay
beneath the skin, the robust tan,
or feel the itch that crawls about
the altered chemistry within the man?

'You look *so* well!'

So what did you expect?
A skeleton in squandered tissue
stagnant with neglect
sustained by dregs
and walking,
walking, just,
on feeble legs?

'*You* look *so* well!'

And now I'm wondering,
how you can tell.
Is it the conspicuous absence
of anticipated smell?
Or something triggered by the eyes,
the brush of cheek, the tepid hand,
that altered what you'd come to understand

and modulates that tone
of caught surprise?

'You   look   so   well!
You really do,
and that's the truth.
I didn't know.'

The truth that turns the face
to show, as you detect,
a trace of joy
embedded where the heart
could not destroy with feeling
what the hurt was eager to embrace:
that still, enduring dignity of grace.

Memo to Myself, Living

Look.
Look.
Look.

Look again.

Then,
without gall,
stripped of protective raiment
and the past's tight artifice,

look once more.

Remission

I keep my hair short,
breathe long,

count tonight's
benevolent stars,
not yesterday's chickens;

In the wet
beneath the trees,
I shelter
from the possibility
of sun,

mindful of
how seeds
may fall.

In Plain View

Only the leaf
holding, holding
trembling
on its brief umbilical
and I
gazing
beyond, beyond
and the sky turning.

Chemo Brain

Once I could juggle
with thirteen troubles
all in a huddle at one time;
but now I struggle,
my brain befuddles
when two things muddle in a line.

I can't complain.

It used to be
the art of juggling
called for tense meticulous care;
but now, you see,
while I am guddling
forgotten things hang in the air.

Chemo Brain: Appointment

You think you've got it set and clear:
5.30 then, sure I'll be there!
Then someone asks you: *was it 4?*
And, though you've just gone out the door,
you're thrown in doubt and, after a pause,
soon you're convinced that 4 it was.

So you roll up early, they look in surprise,
and after a moment you realise,
saying: *Don't mind me!* with a nonchalant air
I always leave plenty of time to spare!

Out Of The Passive Voice

Be patient, patient,
you're indisposed,
be rested, tested,
diagnosed.

Be patient, patient,
be analysed,
scheduled, admitted,
hospitalised;
undergo procedures,
treatments, surgeries,
interventions, therapies,
operations, scans,
dialyses, centeses,
plasties, ectomies,
oscopies, ostomies,
ographies, otomies,
intubations, cannulations,
transplantations,
anaesthetisations,
have tumours reduced,
remissions enlarged,
receive the prognosis,
and be discharged.

The patient patient
has aspirations.

Some time soon,
when my cloud cuckoo calls
to the listening ear,

after consultations I understand,
I'll harness the energy of my fear
and check myself into my chosen ward,
initiate treatments I'll will to succeed,
engage the procedures we decide,
joined and informed body and mind,
realise interventions,
work at therapies,
make operations
and meditations
knowing and feeling
we activate healing,
being and doing,
doing and being.

Gratitude for Whatever

I can't be anything other
than grateful.

What's the point?

Anger?
Hatred?
Jealousy?
Lamentation?

It is too hard work.

Gratitude is the point
of least resistance.

The World We Have

The world we have
is good:
the morning sun,
we have no other.

Grey rains feeding us;
that cooling waft of air;
the blackbird's song;
can we reject them?

Catching the complicit smile
of any someone on the street;
the touch of lips;
a shared umbrella;
all the warmth that spreads
through one extended hand.

The moment when I cease
to struggle with my chaos of despairs,
a voice is calling:
Where are you travelling, friend?
How far have you come?

At Oldshoremore
(for Mary Ogilvy d. 18 May 2011)

Mother, can you hear me through the wind?
I listen for the solace of a voice
amongst the marram grasses in the dunes.
The gap grows, and the slow, receding tide
relinquishes the washed sheet of the beach.
I hear the sea birds keening round those lines
of failing waves advancing to retreat.
I feel you, but the words no longer reach.

Along the shore the bedrock's been exposed:
a chaos of contortions, whorled, contused,
flesh-pink through black, the chance of crystal chemistry
and change, its distance cold as that last kiss
which took the warmth out of my lips
and gave me stone, and this to wonder at.

No Hero

I didn't choose courageousness: who would?
Courage signified a dread come looming,
fallen out of circumstance, entombing
down a slippery-sided well. I could
have held my breath and hid beneath a shame
of murky waters. But I knew I must
not flinch to scale that concave wall, if just
to bear the hollow meaning of a name.

I climbed because I knew it must be done,
and not to revel in the accolades:
those rung endorsements from that cheering throng
of gazers, praising once the thing was won.
It wasn't me who opted to be brave:
in truth, the call of starlight was too strong.

Just a Check-Up

Was that a night-sweat, or has spring arrived
and now it's time to change the winter quilt?

Is *all* this weight-loss due to exercise
I'm doing to assuage a sense of guilt?

Something *is* niggling under my arms;
and cramps are tying knots inside my calves.

I sense my lymph nodes sending out alarms
to indicate the have-not changed to have.

I eschew my future, grip hard to my past,
so tentatively touch my present,
thinking, if this time should be the last,
how I might live it as a time transcendent.

We are the tagged survivors of the fall
who wait, in passing sunlight, for recall.

State of the Art

It's the state of the art. He's surrounded by
the attendant forms of programmed machines.
Stooping before him, their console heads bowed
with functionary, charted smiles,
they proclaim his ongoing god-given right to live
with a fanfare of obsequious bleeps.
They've no authority to recognise
he's always otherwise detained in sleep.

I approach him in his new realm of tubes
and wires, pressure gauges, ventilators,
urinary catheters, drips and bags.
My fingers fresh with rubbed in alcohol,
I cup his hand below the cannula
and brush my lips in tribute with a kiss.

That's the Point

It was well before the beginning of the end;
somewhere between the end of the beginning
and the progression after the direction had been set,
but prior to the turn and the revelation
of how it would proceed towards
the inevitable conclusion.

We didn't recognise it until it had happened;
we saw it, but by then it was too late,
and the ending had already begun
before the beginning had had time to take
and we'd awakened to what had really been going on.

It was unforgiving; so wickedly obvious.
If only they'd seen it coming.
But they didn't, and that's the point.

Final Consultation

She told him he was *normal, free to go;*
the world's your oyster – she described it well:
something soft and vulnerable in a shell,
prone to contamination, slow to grow
its random irritation into pearl.

Discharged, released, induced to *pick things up*
where he'd left off, as if his dwindling cup
had been refilled with light to wash the world.

He hesitated, conjured fantasies
of what it would be like to walk away
into before, revisit the places
and the faces he'd known previously,
framed in their meanings from another time,
returned to normal, diagnosis: fine.